# THE ONE

## GREAT STORIES: HIGH BEGINNER

## SUE LEATHER

WAYZGOOSE PRESS

Edited by Stella Mulford

Cover by getcovers.com

Printed in the United States

ISBN: 978-1-961953-25-3

# CONTENTS

# BEFORE YOU READ

## Vocabulary Notes

This book is for beginning-level readers. Almost all the vocabulary is at the A2 level. However, some intermediate vocabulary is used too.

You can learn these words before you read, or you can check this section again while you read. You can also use a dictionary while you read, or guess what words mean by thinking about the rest of the sentence. However, we recommend reading through the example sentences and notes below before beginning the book, no matter what vocabulary strategy you use.

## Sports Vocabulary

This book is about the sport of basketball. There are five players on a basketball **team**, and a **coach** who helps them. You can play basketball outside, but teams often practice inside in a **gym**, a large room for playing sports in a school or at a club. Players keep their clothes and sports equipment in a **locker** (a metal cabinet) in the **locker room**.

A locker room in a gym. Three lockers are open.

Basketball is played on a **court**, a rectangular area marked with lines. At either end is a **basket** a on a tall pole. Around the basket is a **net**. To score a point, a player **shoots** (throws) the ball into the basket. The past tense is **shot**, which can also be a noun. You can tell a basketball player, "Nice shot!" if they score a point by shooting the basketball into the basket.

Two basketball teams playing on a court. One player is shooting the ball toward the basket.

Basketball is a **competitive** sport. That means every game is a **competition**. One team will win, and one team will lose. Teams who **compete** against each other are called **rivals**. Two people can also be *rivals* if they are both trying to win the same game.

～

To get better, basketball players **practice** and **train**. These words have a similar meaning, but they're not exactly the same. You *practice* the same movement over and over again.

In basketball, you can *practice* shooting, for example. **Training** is more general. You can *train* to be a better basketball player by running, jumping, and *practicing* shooting baskets. Some players *train* by going to the gym and lifting **weights**—heavy pieces of metal.

In school, coaches give **awards** or **trophies** to the best players. A *trophy* is a kind of award that looks like a large cup.

A woman holding a trophy and an award

## Discussion questions

Talk about these questions with a friend, or think about them to yourself.

1. Do you play any sports? Which ones?
2. Do you like to watch any sports? Which ones?
3. How often do you practice something (for example, a sport, music, a hobby)?
4. Do you have any rivals? What are you rivals in? (For example: a sport, in a school class, for friends.)

～

# 1

## JADE

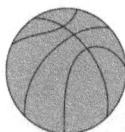

"Great work, Jade," said Coach Paul Dixon. "You really played very well this evening."

"Thanks, Coach Dixon!" Jade replied. She put her towel around her neck and took a drink of water from her water bottle. Jade and her coach walked off the basketball court at Vancouver's Downtown Gym. The gym was the home of the Vancouver Eagles Basketball Club. Paul Dixon was the club coach, and Jade practiced there three times a week.

"You're a good point guard. A *very* good one." said Coach Dixon. "I'm happy you came here from Calgary!"

"Thank you!" Three months ago, Jade's mother, a professor, got an important job at a university in Vancouver. So the family decided to move from Calgary to Vancouver.

"And I'm very happy you joined our club." Dixon laughed. "It's much better than the Vancouver Bears."

Jade laughed too. "I'm sure it is!" she said. The

Vancouver Bears and the Vancouver Eagles were the two biggest basketball teams in the city. Jade knew that the two teams were rivals.

"I want to talk to you about something," said the coach.

Jade and Coach Dixon sat down on a bench at the side of the court. The other girls in the team walked to the locker room.

"Jade," said Dixon, "the thing is… I think that…."

Jade suddenly remembered the time. She looked at her watch. It was seven o'clock. She had to get home! "Oh! Sorry, Coach, I can't now. It's late," she said. She stood up quickly. "How about Thursday? We can talk after practice."

"Well, OK," said Dixon. "Let's talk Thursday." He stood up too. "Is everything OK?" he added.

"Uh… yeah, great," Jade said as she ran to the locker room. "I just have to go."

Jade changed quickly, then ran to get the bus home to West Vancouver. On the bus, she felt worried. She knew that her mom and dad were waiting for her. As she opened the red front door of her house, she began to feel unhappy. When she walked into her house, she felt *very* unhappy. These days, the only time she felt happy was when she was playing basketball.

"You're late again, Jade!" Beth Mason came to the door and looked at her daughter. Jade could see that her mother was angry.

"Sorry, Mom," said Jade. "It's the bus. It takes…"

"Your dinner…"

"I'll eat it now," said Jade.

"And what about your homework?"

"I... I'll do it later tonight, or tomorrow before I go to school."

Her mother didn't look happy with Jade's answer. "You know, Jade," she said, "it's just basketball and more basketball with you right now. That's all you want to do! What about school?"

Her mom was always like this. She just didn't understand Jade's love of basketball. "But Mom..."

"And what about your future? You can't just do sports, you know. What about going to university?"

"I'm only fifteen, Mom," said Jade. "I have three years to think about university."

"Yes," said Jade's mom, "but you have to study hard now. Your schoolwork is so much more important than the Vancouver Eagles. Don't you see that?"

"I told you before, Mom. I can go to university *and* play basketball!" said Jade.

"You're not being very sensible, Jade!" said Beth. "You don't understand this now, you're too young, but... oh, I don't know. Maybe if your father talks to you. Jack!" she called her husband.

But Jade didn't want to talk to her father or her mother. She ran upstairs to her bedroom and closed the door. She lay on her bed and thought about her ex-girlfriend, Devon, back in Calgary. She thought about all her other friends too. Oh, she could text them, even call them, but it just wasn't the same now that she was in Vancouver. She couldn't go to the café with them or to the mall. She couldn't just hang out. She didn't have anyone she could talk to about her parents. There was nobody she could just talk to!

She put her face in her pillow and started to cry. She missed her friends so much!

## 2

## THE ONE

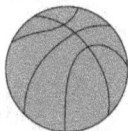

"The thing is, Jade," said Coach Dixon when they talked on Thursday, "not everyone can be a great point guard, but I think you can."

"Really?"

"Yes, really. You're shorter than most basketball players, and you know how to do the job."

Jade knew that the point guard had the most important job on the team, because she had to control the game. She was important because she followed the coach's plan for the game.

"Yes," the coach went on, "you're smaller and faster than most other players."

The point guard was not as tall as the other players on the team, but she was very important.

"I really think you could be The One," said Dixon.

The point guard was sometimes called *The One*. The most famous basketball players in history were point guards: Magic Johnson, Steph Curry, Sue Bird, Caitlin

Clark. Jade was quiet, surprised at the idea that she could be as good as they were. Was she really good enough to be The One?

"So I want to say," continued Dixon, "that I think you really can do it. Maybe you could even be on the national team one day."

"Wha..." Jade didn't know what to say. *Play for Canada?* "You mean..."

Coach Dixon smiled. "Yes, I mean play for Canada. If you practice hard, work hard, I think you could do it!"

Jade felt happy. Her coach in Calgary was OK, but he wasn't as good as Coach Dixon. Coach Dixon had much more experience. He could help Jade be a better player.

They sat for a while, talking. Then Coach Dixon left, and Jade walked into the locker room to change.

~

In the locker room, one of the other girls on the team, Stacy, was still there. Stacy was tall and slim, with short brown hair, and Jade thought she looked nice. Really nice.

Stacy smiled at Jade. "You're very good," she said. "I'm so happy you joined the club."

"Oh, thanks. I think it's a really good club. And Coach Dixon's great!

"Yes," Stacy said. "He's a good guy and a fantastic coach! I really learn a lot from him."

"I agree."

"I've seen you around school, too," said Stacy.

"Oh?" Jade replied. "I haven't seen you, but I'm new..."

Neither of them said anything for a moment. Stacy looked like she wanted to talk to Jade. Jade waited.

"Uh…" Stacy said finally, "maybe you want to go to Jojo's one day after practice? They have really good cakes." She gave Jade a big smile.

Jojo's was a famous café downtown, and Jade wanted to go there. But evenings were impossible.

"Oh, I can't go after practice… sorry." Jade didn't want to explain to Stacy about her mom and dad.

"Well, what about Saturday morning?" Stacy asked, still smiling. "Or after school one day?"

"Oh, yes!" said Jade. "'That would be lovely. Maybe this Saturday morning?"

"Eleven o'clock?"

"Great!"

"It's a date! I'll see you at Jojo's at eleven on Saturday morning!"

When Jade got on the bus to go home that evening, she felt happy. There were so many nice things! The Vancouver Eagles was a much better club than the one in Calgary. And Coach Dixon was really great—he saw that she was good and wanted her to be better. She liked her classmates, and the other girls on the team were nice too, nice and friendly. Especially Stacy.

# 3

## A GOAL

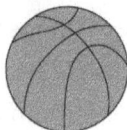

The next week, before practice, Coach Dixon called the team together.

"Listen up, everyone," the coach said to the girls. "I have something to say before we start. Something important."

The gym became quiet.

"Today is May 1st," he went on, "and in June, we choose our club Player of the Year."

The girls looked at each other.

"What does that mean?" asked one of the new players.

"What does that mean? Well, we send our Player of the Year to the national training camp for juniors in the summer," he explained. "The club pays for everything, so it's a fantastic opportunity for one of you. Any questions?"

"When is the summer camp this year?" asked Candace King, one of the girls on the team.

"The last week of July," answered Coach Dixon.

"Where is it?" asked Grace Lang, another of the players.

"This year it's in Kelowna. You can take the bus. It's a long trip, but there will be other basketball players on the bus to talk to. Anything else?"

No one spoke.

"At the camp, you'll meet really good players from other clubs," he went on, "and you'll get excellent coaching. You'll become a much better basketball player."

"So this month," he finished, "I want to see every one of you work hard. Harder than ever before. Show me how good you are! Now, let's practice!"

~

Later, after practice, Jade and Stacy walked to the bus stop together. They were good friends now. They always talked a lot. They liked many of the same things. The listened to the same music, and they liked the same books and movies. They really got on well together.

When they got to the bus stop, Stacy suddenly turned to Jade.

"What do you think about what the coach said?"

"About what?"

"About the Player of the Year, of course!"

"Oh, I don't know," said Jade. "I..."

"Well, listen, Jade, I think you can be Player of the Year," Stacy said.

"Oh... really?" Jade laughed. "But there are some really good players at the club."

"That's true," said Stacy, "but you're the best!"

"Ha!" said Jade. "You're saying that because you like me!"

Stacy laughed too. "Yes, I like you, it's true," she said. "I like you very much. But you *are* the best player!"

~

At home, in her bedroom, Jade lay on her bed and thought. She thought about what Stacy said. She thought about Coach Dixon. He also said she was really good.

Everything was going so well, she thought. Now she had friends at school and at the club. Coach Dixon was great. There was Stacy, too… Now Jade didn't miss her friends in Calgary so much.

The only bad thing in her life was that her mom and dad didn't understand her. They didn't want her to play basketball. They were angry with her when she came home late from practice. They didn't believe that she could be good at school *and* be good at basketball. They didn't know how much she loved the sport.

*Perhaps if I become Player of the Year,* she said to herself, *that will show Mom and Dad that I'm really serious about basketball—and that I'm really good! Perhaps then they won't be mad at me all the time.*

Jade sat up. She took her notebook and a pen from her bedside table. She opened the notebook at the page for May 1st, and wrote in large letters:

**Goal:** To be the Vancouver Eagles Player of the Year.

She had just one month!

## 4

## RIVAL

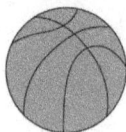

Jade trained hard, even harder than before.

Every morning, she got up early to run around her neighborhood before breakfast. She went to practice early and worked in the gym before the other players came. On the basketball court, she practiced her shots over and over again.

She trained hard at basketball, but she also studied hard at school. She didn't want her mom and dad to get mad. She didn't tell them about her goal.

After a week of work, Jade could feel that she was improving. She was stronger and faster than before.

Coach Dixon could see it, too. "Great work, Jade," he said to her. "You're really getting better every day."

One afternoon after school, Jade and Stacy went to Jojo's.

They drank juice and ate chocolate cake. Jade told Stacy about her goal and her training.

"And how's it going?" asked Stacy.

"It's going really well," Jade said. "I think I'm getting better."

"That's great!" said Stacy. Then she thought for a moment and said, "Be careful, though, Jade."

"What do you mean?" asked Jade.

"Watch out for Candace."

"Candace?"

"Well, Candace is working hard, too. You know that she also wants to win Player of the Year, don't you?"

"Oh? I didn't really think about it. I know that she's a good player…" Jade knew that Candace also wanted to be the club's point guard.

"Yes, she is, " said Stacy, "but she's also mean. I know her. If she thinks that you're going to win, she may try something."

Jade laughed. "Oh, come on, Stacy," she said, "what can she do?"

Stacy didn't laugh. "Well, like I say, just be careful. I know her well. Watch her. She's mean, and she's jealous of you."

∼

A few days later, Coach Dixon came up to Jade after training. He looked unhappy. "Can I talk to you, Jade?"

"Of course. What's up, Coach?"

"Is it true that you're training with the Vancouver Bears, as well as with this club?"

"What? Who told you that?"

"Never mind. Is it true?"

"No, it isn't true, Coach," said Jade. "Of course it isn't true!"

Coach Dixon could see that Jade was upset by what he said. "Well, OK," he said, "I believe you. But if you train with another club..."

"Coach, I'm only training with the Vancouver Eagles," Jade said, her face red. And with that, she walked quickly to the locker room.

~

Jade was mad. *Who told Coach Dixon this lie? And why did they do that?* She sat in the locker room and thought.

At home, Jade sent Stacy a text.

> Hi! Can we talk later? After dinner?

> Sure!

Jade went downstairs and ate dinner. Half an hour later, she went to her room, called Stacy, and told her about what Coach Dixon said.

"I don't know why he thinks that!" said Jade.

"I told you, Jade," said Stacy. "It's Candace!"

"But..."

"I'm sure of it," said Stacy. "Candace has been at the club a long time, and you're new. She's jealous. She and her friend Grace probably said something so the coach could hear it. That's the kind of thing they do."

"I don't believe it," said Jade.

"That's because you're nice," Stacy answered. "But believe me, Candace will do anything—*anything*—to be the Vancouver Eagles Player of the Year!"

## 5

# ACCIDENT?

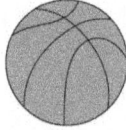

For the next week, Jade's training went really well. As usual, she got up early to run around her neighborhood before school. She went to practice early and worked hard in the gym, lifting weights and building her body. On the basketball court, she practiced her shots again and again. She got stronger and stronger. She felt good. She forgot about what Stacy said about Candace. She forgot everything except her training.

A week later, Jade was training at the club. She was playing hard, moving around the basketball court very quickly. The other girls were playing hard, too. Everybody was trying to show the coach that they were good.

It was the middle of the game. Jade was running fast to the basket to receive the ball from another player. Candace suddenly ran toward her and pushed Jade very hard with her shoulder. Jade fell. In seconds she was on the floor, holding her ankle.

"Aagh!" Jade cried out in pain. Her face was white.

"Stop, everyone!" The coach stopped the game. He came running over to Jade. "Are you hurt, Jade?" he asked.

Jade nodded her head. "I think so... It's my ankle. Is it broken?"

Coach Dixon carried her off the court. He looked carefully at Jade's ankle.

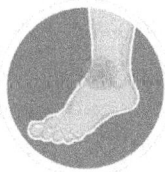

A hurt ankle

"Stacy, get a bag of ice from the locker room," he said. A minute later, Stacy came running back with the ice.

"Well, it isn't broken," said the coach, putting the bag of ice on Jade's ankle. "But you won't be able to play for at least a week. Don't run or walk. You have to rest your ankle."

"A week!" Jade cried out. She only had two more weeks until the coach decided who was the Player of the Year!

"You have to rest it," Coach Dixon said. His voice was calm. "It's just a week."

Jade shook her head. *A week!* That was about twenty hours of training—of running in the morning, of gym work, of playing basketball!

"OK, everyone," Coach Dixon called out to the players. "That's enough for tonight. You can go home. I'll see you on Tuesday." He took the ice off Jade's ankle and put a bandage around it.

"When you get home," he said to Jade, "rest it, and put ice on it often."

Jade nodded. "OK."

Then Stacy helped her to walk to the locker room.

In the locker room, Stacy walked up to Candace. She was really mad. "That was you!" she shouted at her. "*You* pushed Jade. You wanted to hurt her!"

"It was an accident!" said Candace.

"Huh!" said Stacy. She pointed her finger at Candace. "Nobody believes that. You're jealous because you know Jade's a better player than you. You know that she's going to be Player of the Year!"

"Oh, shut up, Stacy!" said Grace, Candace's friend. "Just because she's your girlfriend! Anyone can see it was an accident."

"You..." Stacy turned towards Grace.

"Please, everyone," said Jade in a loud voice. "Please don't fight."

～

Outside, Stacy and Jade walked together to the bus stop.

"Maybe it's not so bad," said Stacy. "After all, it's only a week."

"It's terrible, Stacy," said Jade. "A whole week without training!"

"Come on, Jade. You know it will be OK."

"It's all finished, Stacy!" said Jade. "Now I'm never going to be Player of the Year!"

# 6

## A DECISION

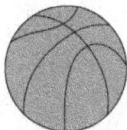

The pain in Jade's ankle was very bad. On the bus home with Stacy, she sat and looked out of the window at the rain. She wanted to cry. She felt terrible.

"What happened?" asked her mom as Jade walked through the door.

"Oh, just an accident."

"Oh Jade, I'm sorry."

"Thanks, Mom."

"But, you know, basketball is such a dangerous sport," her mom went on, shaking her head.

"No, it isn't, Mom," said Jade. She tried to speak calmly.

"But look at you."

"Accidents happen sometimes. They happen in every sport."

"Hmm. But what about school? How will you get there? How will you be able to walk around there?"

"You're just worried about school?" asked Jade. "You're

just thinking about school?" She looked at her mother angrily.

"No, I didn't mean…"

A pair of crutches

"I'm going to my room now," Jade said. "Don't worry about school. Stacy's dad will give me a ride to school tomorrow with Stacy. And after school, Stacy will take me to get a crutch that will help me to walk."

Jade got some ice from the kitchen. Then she went to her bedroom and lay on her bed. She didn't want to talk to her parents, and she didn't want to eat dinner.

That night, Jade didn't sleep a lot. She kept thinking about what happened at the club. She thought about the push from Candace. She saw it again and again in her head. She didn't want to believe that Candace wanted to hurt her. But by the morning, she was sure that Stacy was right. Candace really *did* want to hurt her. She remembered the way Candace looked at her. First Candace told Coach Dixon that Jade was playing with the Vancouver Bears, and then this! She really *did* want to stop Jade from being Player of the Year!

∽

In the morning, early, Jade sent a text to Stacy.

> I've been thinking all night. I think you're right about Candace. I think she wants to stop me.

A few minutes later, Stacy replied.

> Yes, she does!

> But what can I do about it?

> I think you have to talk to Coach Dixon. Candace is dangerous!

> But what am I going to say?

> Just tell him what you told me. I'm sure he'll listen. He knows about Candace, I'm sure! See you in fifteen minutes. We can talk later.

∾

"If what you say is true, Jade," the coach said when Jade called him later that day, "I really must ask her to leave the club. This is very serious."

"But the thing is, Coach," Jade replied, "I think Candace is jealous. She's been at the club a long time, and I'm new. We are both point guards. I understand why she feels that way."

"Hmmm." Coach Dixon listened. And he thought. "You may be right. She's a good player like you, and I know she wants to be the best player in the club."

"And you know that if you ask her to leave the club," Jade said, "she'll just go to the Vancouver Bears."

Coach Dixon wasn't happy at the thought of Candace at the Vancouver Bears.

"Maybe there's another way," said Jade.

At the end of their talk, Coach Dixon and Jade agreed on the best thing to do.

"I'll talk to Candace," said Coach Dixon.

## 7

## A PERFECT EVENING

"You *must* come!" Jade told her parents at the beginning of June. "It's the most important part of the year for the club. You can meet my friends and the other parents. And they're going to announce the Player of the Year!"

At last, her mom and dad decided to come to the club party. There were a lot of people there: the coach, players, sisters and brothers, parents. There was a reporter there, too, from a local newspaper. Her job was to write about the event and take photos.

Before the awards, everyone walked around the room, eating sandwiches and cakes, and drinking coffee, talking to each other. Jade saw Coach Dixon talking to her mom and dad for about ten minutes. Afterward, she could see that her parents seemed happy. She asked herself what her coach said to them.

Then Coach Dixon asked for quiet, and he started speaking. He began to give out the awards and trophies. There were awards for different things: best team player, fastest runner, best defense. Everyone clapped as the players received their awards. But everyone knew that the biggest award was at the end. They waited impatiently for Player of the Year.

"Now, this year I have something special," the coach said finally.

The room was quiet.

"This year we have not just one, but two Players of the Year!"

Now there were whispers in the crowd.

"And those players are..."

More whispers.

"Jade Mason and Candace King!"

Now everyone in the room clapped and cheered very loudly.

"This year, both players are going to the summer camp for national juniors!" Coach Dixon finished.

Jade and Candace walked up to get their awards. He gave each of them a large silver trophy. All the parents and the players took photos. The reporter took lots of photos, too.

Jade looked at Candace. Was she happy that they were both Players of the Year? Jade didn't know.

But a few moments later, Candace walked up to Jade. "Jade, I'm really happy that we'll be at summer camp together," she said.

"Me too!" Jade laughed. "It's going to be fun!"

Then Candace looked serious. "And I'm really sorry about everything..."

Jade smiled, and they both hugged.

Then Jade's mom and dad found her. They both looked happy.

"We're very proud of you," said her dad.

"Yes," said her mom. "We are so proud, darling!"

"But…"

"We can see that you're very good at basketball," explained her dad.

"And your school grades are good too," said her mom, smiling.

"And," said her dad, "most of all, you were very kind. You showed kindness and understanding in a very difficult situation. The coach told us everything."

"Oh!" Jade was surprised and happy. *A perfect evening,* she thought. There was just one thing missing. She left her parents and found Stacy.

"I want to ask you something," Jade said.

"What?"

"Is it true what Grace said?"

Stacy looked at Jade. "What did she say?"

"That I'm your girlfriend."

Stacy laughed. "Yes, you are."

∾

# AFTER YOU READ

## Discussion

Talk about these questions with a classmate, or think or write about them by yourself.

1. Do you think Candace tried to hurt Jade? Why?
2. Jade asked Coach Dixon to let Candace be a Player of the Year with her. Do you think that was the right thing to do? Why or why not?
3. Do you think Candace and Jade will be friends now?
4. Why did Jade's parents change their minds about basketball? Do you agree with them?
5. What are some good things about competitions for teenagers? What are some bad things?

## What Happens Next?

It's next summer. Candace and Jade are at the summer camp in Kelowna. They are working hard and getting better at basketball. They play on different camp teams. Are they friends? Write a letter from Jade to Stacy, explaining how she feels about Candace now. Then write a letter from Candace to Grace, explaining how she feels about Jade.

## Sports Heroes

Who are some important sports players from your country? What sports do they play? Do you ever watch their games? Read about them online. Then tell a friend about them, or write a paragraph.

## Basketball and Entertainment

The Harlem Globetrotters are a famous basketball team that entertains people with very good playing and special tricks. Watch some of their performances on their YouTube channel, https://www.youtube.com/@HarlemGlobetrotters

## WHAT TO READ NEXT

Here are some more books at the same level as *The One*. You can find information about all of these and more on your website at

https://wayzgoosepress.com/graded-readers/

~

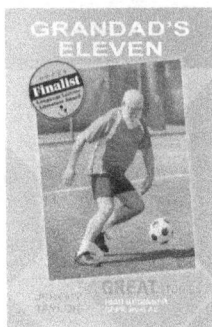

13-year old Ryan doesn't want to visit his grandparents. He's not interested in old people. Old people are boring! He wants to play computer games.

His best friend Ashraf misses his grandparents—they're in Egypt, and he lives in England now. So he goes to visit Ryan's grandparents. Both Ashraf and Albert, Ryan's grandfather, love football. Soon Ashraf agrees to be the coach of Albert's new football team, Grandad's Eleven.

Ryan feels like he is losing his friend. Ashraf can't understand why Ryan won't help him with the team. And Albert? He's worried about the game next week. Grandad's Eleven has only ten players!

*Grandad's Eleven* is a short story for readers who like sports, friends, family... and surprises.

～

Maria wonders about the sad man who sits in the café where she works. Who is he? Where is he from? What does he do?

One day, she talks to him, and is surprised to learn that he is Georgie Goode, the famous football player! But he's not famous now, and he's not playing football now. What happened?

And so Georgie tells her his story...

A story about sports, friendship, and playing fair.

～

"This is a true story! It happened to a friend of a friend of mine …"

Do you know the story of the silver hook? The mysterious hitchhiker? The babysitter who gets some troubling phone calls? How about the story of Hanako-san, a Japanese schoolgirl who some say appears in school bathrooms? These are all examples of urban legends: creepy stories that people have told—and retold—to their friends.

∿

Nick Mason is a journalist. He wants to write exciting stories—and now there is one. A beautiful girl was killed at a party. Who was she? Who killed her? And why?

But Nick wants to do more than just write the story. Because he knew this girl…

A classic-style detective story set in Los Angeles in the 1930s. For readers who love glamour, danger, and mystery.

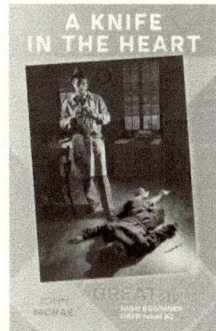

∿

And more! Reading for pleasure helps your learn English while enjoying yourself.

# ABOUT THE AUTHOR

Sue Leather has a background as teacher, trainer, and consultant in English Language Teaching. She has been writing original learner fiction since 1990 and has some 35 books in print with a range of publishers. She has twice won a Language Learner Literature Award, for *Dead Cold* (Cambridge University Press) and *Ask a Friend* (Stand For Readers). She was Joint Series Editor for *Page Turners* (Cengage/National Geographic).

## ABOUT THE PUBLISHER

Wayzgoose Press publishes a variety of books for both teachers and students of English, including self-study guides, textbooks, and more volumes in the *Great Stories* and the *Big Ideas* reader series. Find our full range of titles on our web page at

http://wayzgoosepress.com

To be notified about the release of new titles and special contests, events, and sales from Wayzgoose Press, please sign up for our mailing list (find the sign-up link on the website). We send email infrequently, and you can unsubscribe at any time.

www.ingramcontent.com/pod-product-compliance
Lightning Source LLC
Chambersburg PA
CBHW021119020426
42331CB00004B/553